A TASTE OF

Saffron

Printed and Bound by Gomer Press Limited, 2016
Llandysul Enterprise Park, Llandysul, Ceredigion SA44 4JL
www.gomerprinting.co.uk

A CIP record for this book is available from the British Library
ISBN 978-0-995 6580-0-4
www.houseofsaffron.co.uk

Acknowledgements

This book was inspired by the extraordinary history of Saffron Walden and the fact that due to cost, and poor substitutes/adulterations, saffron was eventually replaced by cocoa, vanilla and turmeric which led to this mystical spice falling into disfavour. Saffron is a unique spice with a hard to define flavour but when added to dishes makes it special and worth savouring. It imbues the dish with a golden hue and adds a bitter sweet flavour.

My thanks to my husband, Paul for his idea of putting saffron back into Saffron Walden, his constant support and continually challenging me to the next level.

To Vanessa Brewer whose inimitable photographic style portrays the colour and appeal of the saffron dishes so beautifully. To Kimberley Bouland who created the saffron logo and sketched all the Saffron Walden destinations from her personal perspective and experiences moving to Saffron Walden.

A note on the publishers, Gomer Press: I discovered them on the Round the Coast of Britain in E-type Jaguars, a 19 day fundraising event for Prostate cancer. A four generation family run business that could meet my requirements to publish before Christmas, 2016.

My thanks also to Dr Sally Francis, a botanist who was the first to research and reintroduce Crocus Sativus as a saffron crop, cultivated in Norfolk since the early nineties. Sally was an inspiration with her passion and deep knowledge and experience with saffron.

Finally, Malcolm White, a 34 year veteran Town Clerk of Saffron Walden whose comprehensive knowledge and insights of the chronological history of Saffron Walden that helped shape the book.

Foreword

Saffron Walden is probably unique in taking its prefix from a spice. The fact that it does so shows the importance of that crop to the town. Used largely as a dye for the resurgent woollen industry of Suffolk, there can be no question that the wealth of the town in the 15th – 17th century was directly attributable to that crop and is perhaps most beautifully witnessed in our magnificent Parish Church of St Mary's. Saffron, obtained from the Crocus Sativus, was an incredibly valuable, though somewhat unreliable, crop. Its value fluctuated from as little as 12 shillings a pound in 1548, to over £4 in 1665 with wild variations in between. The reasons for this were varied - failed crops, vogues of fashion, foreign imports – all made Saffron an unreliable crop and by the early 1700's the crop had largely died out.

But during its heyday the towns pride in its crop and its significance to the local economy is reflected in the gifts of Saffron made to monarchs on their visits to Audley End with Elizabeth, James I, Charles I, Charles II, William III and George III all being presented with saffron. The pride in Saffron was perhaps best shown, that although the crop was no longer being grown in the time of George III, saffron was actually purchased from elsewhere to present to him in his visit in 1777. Today the crocus can still be seen growing in local gardens, giving a little bit of colour to the autumnal period of its flowering.

The influence of Saffron on the development of the town cannot be underestimated. Saffron is still a popular commodity and the mouth tasting recipes in this book show that our ancestors were well aware of its use not just as a dye, but also for its uses in cooking and baking.

- Malcolm White, (Town Clerk 1976 – 2010)

Introduction

A Taste of Saffron contemporizes saffron dishes pairing them with the touristic delights that Saffron Walden has to offer. This book is dedicated to revive the use of saffron in its legacy context of surprising aroma of flame, honey with fresh hay and it's enriching distinct flavor while infusing the dishes with a golden sunshine colour to delight the senses. 30 Tourist destinations are paired with 30 recipes. Each recipe section is colour coded with the saffron palette.

This book is designed with freedom. No set meal plan with drink, mains, sides and desserts. Rather dishes that can work alone or in combination in any setting be it a formal dinner, informal with a pot in the middle of the table to share from the same dish which is symbolical, or packed cold as a picnic to enjoy in Jubilee gardens, Bridge end Gardens or on the Common. Leftovers can take on a new life when paired with new companions. Page through the cakes and biscuits section to page 110 for my favourite delight.

Saffron is valued for its dusty perfume and its brilliance of colour. Pound for pound it is the costliest of spices. Just enough threads on the tip of a knife can scent and gild a dish and turn a simple dish of rice into a meal for a king. Saffron provides a gentle joy to those who treasure the value rather than the price.

Take pause, enjoy the saffron as a way of life not so much as a recipe. Enjoy the delights that Saffron Walden has to offer like the market on a Tuesday or Saturday which dates back centuries where news was discussed, ideas passed on and the saffron appeared from the spice merchants of the Ottoman empire.

RECIPE INDEX

PLACE INDEX

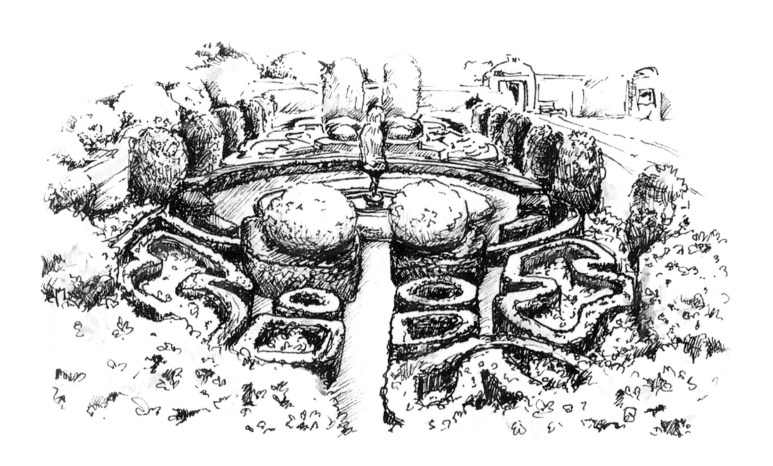

Bridge End Gardens

Located on the north side of town, Bridge End Garden has been described as a hidden gem. It is a beautifully restored Victorian Garden made up of seven small interconnecting gardens and is full of surprises like the magnificent hedge maze. Each area has a different theme: The Dutch Garden, Pavilion, Poets' Corner and Jacob's Well, The Rose Garden, The Wilderness, The Summer House Lawn and The Walled Garden.

There are entrances from Castle Street, past the Fry Gallery and gentle winding Bridge Street with borders leading to the splendid Eagle Gates of the Dutch Garden. It was laid out by the Gibson family in the nineteenth century.

These Grade II listed gardens are open to the public every day free of charge. Careful restoration has replicated gardening techniques and designs typical of the Victorian era and has brought the garden back to its full splendour.

Saffron Milk

After a long day filled with deadlines and chores, it's time to wind down and take pause. This beverage is an age old remedy for just that. The 20 minutes preparation time is just enough to stop thinking about your troubles. Start by deliberately dropping the saffron into the milk. Just watch the threads infuse the milk with glorious colour. Sit in your favourite chair and sip slowly, feel the joy of saffron.

- 6 threads saffron
- 250 ml milk
- 1 tablespoon sugar

Bring all ingredients to the boil.
Remove from heat and infuse saffron threads
for 15 minutes before drinking.

Parish Church of St Mary the Virgin

This lavishly designed structure is the largest church in Essex, with a total length of nearly 200 feet. Overlooking the historic market town, it was built in 1430 under the supervision of John Wastell, who also designed King's College Chapel in Cambridge.

St Mary's is home to a vibrant Christian community. Belonging to the Church of England, we are people of all ages and outlooks whose mission is sharing God's love. Services range from cathedral to café style and our strong musical tradition includes an excellent robed choir. The church is open daily for worship and to welcome visitors to a place where the Christian faith has been celebrated for over 800 years.

Our church is open every day of the year from around 8.30am until dusk or later.

- *Rev David Wilkinson*

Butternut Saffron Soup

Butternut is one of my favourite vegetables. This smooth hearty soup served with fresh crusty bread is a meal on its own.

- 500g butternut peeled and cubed
- 250g chopped potatoes
- 60g chopped onion
- 60g butter
- 600ml milk
- 500ml chicken stock
- 6 threads saffron
- 1 teaspoon parsley
- Salt and pepper

Brown the onion in butter.
Add butternut, potato, milk, and saffron.
Simmer until cooked.
Liquidize, add stock to the mixture.
Add seasoning to taste, sprinkle with parsley.

Swan Meadow Maze

Opened in August 2016, the town's fourth open air maze displays various complementary aspects: As a gateway to the town centre, its internal layout announces that "Saffron Walden Amazes." Natural materials such as reconstituted stone paving and "box" hedging within a woven willow fence and external ground cover planting complement the adjacent trees, duck pond and water meadow. Miniature finger labyrinths and mazes set into planters offer activity opportunities to young children along the twists and turns of its pathways.

-   *John Ready*

Cauliflower Saffron Soup

Server 4 – 6

Cauliflower is freshly available at any market. This creamy soup is simple to make and can be enjoyed all year round.

- 4 cups chicken/vegetable stock
- 8 threads saffron
- 2 tablespoons olive oil
- 1 large onion chopped
- 2 stalks celery, finely chopped
- 2 cloves garlic, chopped
- 1 ½ lb cauliflower, chopped
- 1 medium potato peeled and chopped
- 1 handful of fresh parsley

Heat stock in medium saucepan, add saffron. Remove from heat, allow saffron to infuse. Heat olive oil in medium pot. Add chopped onion and celery, sauté till tender (not brown). Add garlic, cook another minute. Add cauliflower and potato; stir to coat. Add saffron stock, bring to boil. Reduce heat, simmer for 20 minutes. Puree the soup till smooth. Season with salt and pepper, serve garnished with parsley.

Fry Art Gallery

Donated by Francis Gibson in 1856, this building has been revived by well-known 20th and 21st century artists resident in the town or the surrounding districts. Foremost among these artists are Edwin Bawden, Eric Ravilious, Michael Rothenstein, John Aldridge and John Bellany. In 1985, the charitable Fry Art Gallery society was formed with the specific purpose of bringing this building (which was closed for fourteen years) back to life. It now houses 3000 works of art.

Some 30 artists known for their distinctive work who are associated with the town and surroundings have contributed to the gallery's exhibits. The Gallery is managed entirely by volunteers and is accredited by The Arts Council of England as a Public Museum. It is open from April to October. Every year, a different exhibition is drawn from the Gallery's Permanent Exhibition and three temporary exhibitions can be viewed in an adjacent room. Entrance to the Gallery is free. Please check opening times online.

- *Nigel Weaver*

Orange Lentil and Carrot Soup

Lentils are an underrated pulse. They add texture and substance to this soup. Adding saffron to a winter soup reminds us of sunshine of summers past.

- 2 cups orange lentils
- 6 carrots peeled and sliced
- 1 tin tomato and onion mix
- 500ml chicken/vegetable stock
- 6 threads saffron
- Salt and pepper

Cook the lentils and carrots in the stock.
Add the saffron.
When cooked, add with the tomato and onion mix and liquidize.
Return to pot, heat.
Serve with crusty bread and crisp salad.

Old Sun Inn

The Old Sun Inn is a landmark Grade 1 listed building dating back to the 14th century. It is a timbered construction below a pitched tiled roof. The building is especially well known for its "pargetting," the traditional 17th century craft of decorative external plasterwork depicting flowers, ornate birds and geometric patterns and, oddly, even a leg.

Originally built as a merchant's house, it evolved into an inn and for the last 50 years has housed a shop selling antiques and books. Oliver Cromwell is said to have stayed there during the Civil War. The writer John Evelyn and the diarist Samuel Pepys both recorded visits there.

Chickpeas with Saffron, Garlic and Almonds

This Catalan dish uses almonds and saffron that came to Spain with Moors. I like the crunchy golden taste of the dressing.

- 4 tablespoons olive oil
- 4 tablespoons blanched almonds, finely chopped
- 1 clove garlic, finely chopped
- 4 tablespoons fresh breadcrumbs
- 250g dried chick peas, soaked overnight, drained /2x200g tins
- 8 threads saffron
- 3 tablespoons boiling water
- 600ml chicken or ham stock
- Salt and white pepper

Soak saffron threads for 20 minutes in boiling water.
Put chickpeas in a pan, cover with cold water and bring to the boil.
Simmer for 1 ½ hours until soft.
Heat oil in a heavy pan, gently fry the almonds, breadcrumbs and garlic until golden.
(careful not to burn).
Add saffron and water, chickpeas and stock to cover.
Bring back to boil.
Turn down heat, simmer for 20 minutes.
Remove the lid, turn up the heat.
Season and boil until all liquid has evaporated and the almonds and breadcrumbs begin to fry again.
Turn the chickpeas over, browning everything a little.

Castle Street

Castle Street manages to sum up 900 years of history in a single street. It was first laid out when the Castle was built in the 1140s. The present houses dating mainly from the 1490s provided homes for successful artisans and craftsmen. By the 1800s, this was the poorest part of town, with the old houses divided up into smaller units and four pubs in the long street: a riotous and poor community. Gentrification came gradually with the listing of many of the buildings in the 1950s, and by the 1970s and the closing of the last pub. The street now has a picture-postcard beauty and, having come a full circle, its residents once again reflect the same social standing as the people who first lived there over 500 years ago.

- *Sarah Kirkpatrick*

Italian Saffron Rice Cakes

These tasty rice cakes outdo fritters or chips and are versatile as a side, or with a tomato and mozzarella salad or chicken dishes.

- 350g Arborio (risotto) rice
- 1.5 litres of stock (chicken or beef)
- 50g butter
- 3 shallots or 1 medium onion finely chopped
- 6 threads saffron
- Salt and freshly ground pepper

To finish

- 3-4 eggs lightly beaten
- 1 tablespoon grated Parmesan
- Olive oil and 2 tablespoons butter

Soak saffron threads for 20 minutes in boiling water.
Heat the stock and allow to simmer.
Melt half the butter in a large, heavy pan.
Fry gently till golden.
Add the soaked saffron liquid with a ladleful of stock.
Season, simmering until liquid is absorbed. Continue ladleful by ladleful until rice is tender but still nutty at the centre (15 minutes).
Cover and leave to rest 10-15 minutes off the heat till rice grains are separate but juicy.
Allow to cool.
Stir in eggs and Parmesan.
Heat oil and butter in a big frying pan till sizzling.
Drop in spoonfuls of rice mixture, fry till crisp on outside & soft inside.
Place on kitchen paper to drain.

8 Bells

The Eight Bells on Bridge Street is another historic Saffron Walden Inn with 15th and 16th century wings and a projecting first floor jetty. Today, it is a charming Grade II listed half-timbered pub with period decor, a beer garden and a cosmopolitan menu.

It has modern additions and is made up of different elements. The 15th century portion is perpendicular to the road and the 16th Century addition is the ground floor street front. The upper storey projects as a continuous overhang (jetty) to create bigger rooms. The original windows on the ground and first floor have carved sills and are finished with mouldings.

Saffron Pilaf

Saffron Pilaf is an elegant and delicate variant of the Indian Pilau. Serve with poultry.

- 1 ¼ cups long grain rice
- 2 ½ cups chicken stock
- 6 threads saffron
- Salt and freshly ground black pepper
- 2 tablespoons pine nuts, roasted
- 2 spring onions, thinly sliced
- 3 tablespoons fresh parsley, chopped

Wash the rice in 4 changes of water, drain.
Simmer stock in a covered pan.
Add saffron, season, turn off heat
allowing saffron to infuse for 15 minutes.
Add rice, boil, cover then simmer for 15 minutes.
Mix in pine nuts, spring onions & parsley.

Saffron Hotel

Located on High street in the centre of Saffron Walden, this historic 16th century coaching Inn features a charming restaurant, real ale bar and 16 elegant rooms where a warm and friendly atmosphere and delightful ambience makes this an ideal meeting place for families and friends as it has for the last 400 years.

Saffron Rice

A beautiful sunshine coloured dish of rice

- 1 cup brown or white rice
- 6 threads saffron
- A pinch of salt
- Freshly ground pepper
- 2 cups water

Bring the rice, salt, pepper, saffron and water to boil and simmer until cooked.
Drain and steam to separate the grains and make it light and fluffy.

Audley End

Audley End House sits like a marvellous jewel box in a wonderful 18th century Capability Brown landscape. The Jacobean House replaced the Benedictine Abby which had stood there for 400 years before Henry VIII presented it to Thomas Audley in 1538. Audley's grandson, Thomas Howard, Earl of Suffolk, built the present house. Today you can admire the wonderful interiors, pictures and furniture and also see the workings of the House and landscape from the service wing and nursery to the stables and kitchen garden. The house brings to life the history of the families and house staff that made Audley End one of the leading country houses in East Anglia.

- *Sarah Kirkpatrick*

Saffron Spanish New Potatoes

This sunny saffron-scented dish comes from Valencia. The gently cooked onions and the basic Catalan soffrito are the essentials of this dish. It goes well with grilled sardines or fried anchovies.

- 1kg new potatoes
- 6 tablespoons olive oil
- 2 large onions finely sliced
- 500g tomatoes skinned and chopped (or tinned plum tomatoes)
- 1-2 bay leaves
- 12 threads saffron
- 1 small glass white wine
  1 teaspoon of sugar
- Salt and freshly ground pepper

To finish

- 25g almonds blanched and finely chopped
- 2 tablespoons fresh breadcrumbs
- ½ teaspoon cumin seeds
- 2 cloves garlic finely chopped

To serve

- Crisp lettuce leaves, quartered lemons

Heat 4 tablespoons oil in a big pan.
Add onions, fry till golden and soft on gentle heat for 20 minutes.
Add tomatoes, bay leaves and saffron.
Turn up heat, press and soften tomatoes.
Cook until liquid thickens into a rich sauce.
Add potatoes, wine and a bit of water to cover.
Season with salt and pepper.
Bring to boil, cover loosely; simmer till potatoes are tender (20-30 minutes).
Remove lid, boil until liquid evaporates.
Heat remaining oil in a small pan.
Fry almonds and breadcrumbs till crisp and golden.
Sprinkle remaining saffron, cumin seeds and garlic on top. Remove from heat, stir mixture into potatoes.
Serve warm with lettuce and lemons.

Bridge Street

As you come into the town from the north via Windmill Hill and Bridge Street, the view on the horizon, with the majestic Church has remained almost unchanged for 500 years. Every house on the street is a listed building: the houses on both sides of the road at the bottom of the hill were built with oversailing first floors, decorative pargetting and, on one, a good example of brick noggin. Bridge End Gardens, which can be accessed from the street, offers a welcome haven of peace and quiet, as well as the Dutch Garden, Kitchen Garden and Maze.

- *Sarah Kirkpatrick*

Saffron Tomato Confit

Serves 4 - 6

This recipe just looks so lovely simmering with bright red tomatoes, luscious in their soak of saffron and olive oil.

- 450g cherry tomatoes
- 1/3 good olive oil
- 12 threads saffron
- Salt and freshly ground pepper

Halve tomatoes.
Place tomatoes and oil in a medium pan.
Add saffron, salt and pepper. Mix well and heat.
Once the tomatoes blister and oil gets hot, reduce heat and simmer for 60 minutes, stirring every 10 minutes. Remove from heat, cool in the pan.

Saffron Museum

Saffron Walden Museum was opened in 1835 to house the collections of the Saffron Walden Natural History Society. The collecting interests of its founders were encyclopaedic, so alongside the main displays of archaeology, history and natural history of north-west Essex, you will find Egyptology, decorative arts, world cultures and much more. Meet Wallace the lion, excavate in the archaeological sandpit or explore the natural history discovery centre.

- *Carolyn Wingfield*

Catalan Pasta with Almonds, Pork and Saffron

Serves 4

This Moorish pan dish is set in the middle of the table for everyone to help themselves to the portion in front of them, scooping with bread or crisp lettuce leaves, eating neatly from the outside of the pan to the middle.

- 300g vermicelli
- 250g lean pork, cubed
- 3 tablespoons olive oil
- 8 threads saffron
- 2 tablespoons boiling water
- 1 tablespoon blanched almonds
- 2 cloves garlic, chopped
- 1 tablespoon chopped parsley
- 1 tablespoon paprika
- 1 teaspoon cinnamon, ground
- ½ teaspoon ground cloves
- 1 glass white wine
- 1 lemon, grated zest and juice
- 1 large onion, chopped
- 3 large tomatoes, skinned and chopped or tinned plum tomatoes
- 1 small glass water

Soak saffron threads for 20 minutes in boiling water.
Heat 1 tablespoon oil in a small frying pan.
Fry garlic and almonds until golden.
Add parsley, stir till it is crisp and sizzles.
Blend saffron water, lemon juice and zest.
Tip in parsley, garlic and almonds, blend to a paste.
Dilute with wine - set aside.
Heat 2 tablespoons oil in a large frying pan.
Add pork and onion, fry gently until golden,
15-20 minutes.
Push meat and onion aside in the pan, add
the pasta. Sizzle and fry to a rich golden brown.
Add the tomatoes and boil briskly.
Add the water, boil briskly again.
Stir in the almond sauce.
Boil briskly again.
Reduce heat and simmer gently until pasta is tender
and juices have nearly evaporated, about 10 minutes.

Rooftop view of Gibson House

The rich red brick Tudor chimneys swirl upwards in spirals, each one different from the rest. There is a rosette detail decorated on the lead parapet which contrasts with the geometric brickwork. The soft red-tiled roof tilts upwards at different angles. The heavy cast iron downpipes display small medieval towers cast into metal and the Gibson-Tuke initials. Often we are so intent on our errands we simply do not look up. Next time you enter the Town from the Rose and Crown entrance, look up to the rooftops. You'll be surprised at what you see.

Moroccan Braised Chicken with Saffron

Serves 6

This Moroccan dish can also be prepared in a tagine if you have one. The secret lies in the slow cooking allowing the different flavours to infuse the chicken. I like the combination of nuts and spices.

- 6 chicken pieces
- 1 large mild onion, chopped
- 2 tablespoons oil
- 8 threads saffron
- 1 small stick cinnamon
- 1 tablespoon crushed peppercorns
- Salt
- 600ml water
- 2 tablespoons raisins/chopped prunes

Sauce

- 500g red onions chopped
- 2 tablespoons oil
- ½ teaspoon ginger
- ½ teaspoon ground cumin
- 1 tablespoon honey
- 2 tablespoon blanched, toasted almonds

Lightly toast saffron threads in a pan and put to one side.
Lay chicken pieces on a bed of onion in a heavy casserole.
Drizzle with oil.
Add saffron, cinnamon, pepper and a little salt.
Add water, bring to boil.
Add raisins/prunes, cover loosely.
Simmer gently for 40-60 minutes adding a bit more water when necessary.

Sauce

Gently fry sliced onions in oil until soft and golden.
Sprinkle with a little salt, ginger and cumin, stir in honey and boil briskly.
Remove chicken from broth and reserve. Strain the broth back into pot, boil to reduce to 300ml. Stir in the onion mixture, boil briskly.
Serve sauce ladled over chicken portions.

The Castle

The ruined keep of Walden Castle stands in walled grounds which it shares with Saffron Walden Museum, the district museum for north-west Essex. The Norman earls of Essex built the castle around 1140 and turned the Saxon manor of Walden into the medieval market town of Chepyng (or Chipping) Walden, as it was known before it became famous for saffron.

- *Carolyn Wingfield*

Saffron and Paprika Roast Chicken

Serves 4 - 6

This is one of my favourite Sunday roasts. You can also add chopped parsnips, carrots and potatoes to the roasting dish. The vegetables are infused with the saffron/paprika flavor. Alternatively pair with any of the saffron sides dishes.

- 6 threads saffron
- 4 tablespoons boiling water
- 1 free-range chicken
- Paprika
- Salt and pepper to taste

Soak saffron threads for 20 minutes in boiling water.
Place chicken in roasting dish.
Baste chicken with saffron mixture.
Sprinkle liberally with paprika.
Season with salt and pepper.
Roast at 150°C for 3 hours, turning after an hour and pouring the rest of saffron mixture over chicken and sprinkle again with paprika.

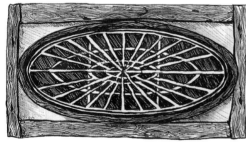

Spider Window

The spider window is well known to residents and tourists to the town. Although the origins of this eye-catching window are not clear, it's present position dates back to the 1930s, when the building stopped being a Convent and half the house was moved, timber by timber, to Sussex. It is something that local people remember drawing in their school days.

Saffron Lamb Stew

This stew is slow cooked till all the vegetables and meat is soft and tender. I sometimes make it in advance and serve it with saffron rice.

- 4 tablespoons oil
- 2 onions, sliced
- 1kg lamb, cubed
- 1 cup whole-wheat flour
- 2 large tomatoes, skinned and chopped
- 3 carrots, diced
- 3 large potatoes, cubed teaspoon crushed coriander
- 6 threads saffron
- Salt
- 3 sprigs rosemary
- ¼ teaspoon grated lemon peel
- Juice of 1 lemon
- Water / vegetable stock
- Parsley, chopped

Fry onions in the oil.
Roll the lamb in the flour, add to onions.
Fry until golden.
Transfer to a casserole dish/slow cooker.
Add all other ingredients, cover with water/stock.
Cook for 1 ½ hours in the oven at 150°C or in the slow cooker, stirring regularly add water if necessary.
Serve with parsley sprinkled on top

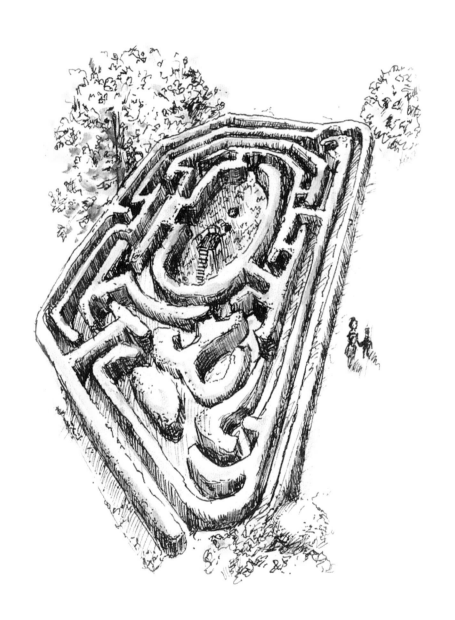

Hedge Maze

Lose yourself in the glades, experience the unexpected and test your orientation skills in the Hedge Maze in Bridge End Garden. If you can, navigate your way to the artwork in the centre of the Maze: a contemporary sculpture by Hamish Horsley entitled 'The Mermaids.'

The Hedge Maze was completed by Francis Gibson in about 1840. It was maintained until 1920. By 1950, as a result of neglect, it had succumbed to invading sycamore trees and by 1980 it was completely overgrown. In 1984, the site was cleared and the new maze was planted in 1986. Extensive restoration in 2004 saw the paths re-established and the wall and entrance gate repaired. Landscaping provided the finishing touches ultimately creating this amazing experience.

Seafood Stew with Saffron

This dish is an operetta of a fish stew, named Zarzuela named after a Spanish operetta called Zaruela first performed in the Zaruela Palace on the outskirts of Madrid, built in the 17th Century on an area covered with brambles or zarzas. This dish was affectionately christened "Little Bramble Palace"- Zarzuela de Pescado. It can be made with fish in season according to your taste.

- 8 threads saffron
- 3 tablespoons boiling water
- 1kg mixed fish (tuna, swordfish, monkfish, squid) cut into chunks
- 2 limes, pulp and juice
- 4 medium onions, chopped
- 4 cloves garlic, chopped
- 225g soaked, cooked chickpeas
- 6-8 tomatoes, skinned and chopped
- 4 bulbs fennel, thinly sliced
- 2-3 yellow peppers, seeded and chopped
- 450g cherry tomatoes
- 300ml white wine
- 300ml fish stock
- Salt and pepper
- Fresh coriander, shredded

Soak saffron threads for 20 minutes in boiling water.

Fry the onions, garlic and fennel in olive oil until soft and translucent (20 minutes).

In a large heavy bottomed casserole, layer half the onion mixture, followed by the fish pieces, tomatoes, chickpeas.

Layer the rest of the onion mixture.

Top this with yellow peppers and cherry tomatoes.

Mix wine, stock, lime juice, salt, pepper with saffron liquid.

Pour this saffron liquid mixture over the casserole.

Bring the whole dish very slowly to the boil which completes the cooking process.

Check that the peppers are soft.

Serve with a sprinkle of shredded coriander.

Cross Keys

The Cross Keys dates back to the late 14th century and is one of the oldest buildings in Saffron Walden. It has a remarkable crown post roof, and was originally a very narrow building, jettied on three sides. In the 16th century a new building was built alongside it in the High Street, blocking up the row that previously ran through on the northern side of the building. For most of its existence, it was a coaching inn and the headquarters of the Post Office. In the late 20th century it became very run down. When the brewery sold it, and after substantial investment, it became a restaurant and boutique hotel, and an old Saffron Walden institution, Molly's Tea Shop, was brought back to life in its old premises in King Street. The building is said to have a ghost, reputedly seen walking in the first floor corridors and bedrooms. The Cross Keys has outdoor seating in the summer and wood fires in the winter.

- *Mike Hibbs*

Shrimp Sautéed with Garlic and Saffron

Serves 4 - 6

This recipe is an easy quick twist on shrimp, perfect on a warm summer's day.

- 3 threads saffron
- 2 tablespoons boiling water
- 575g shrimp, peeled
- ¼ cup oil
- 3 cloves garlic, sliced
- 1 teaspoon cumin, ground
- 1 teaspoon smoked paprika
- Fresh parsley

Soak saffron threads for 20 minutes in boiling water. Add oil to heavy pan, heat. Add garlic, cook till golden.
Add shrimp, cumin, paprika and saffron.
Cook until pink for 5-10 minutes, turning once or twice.

Jubilee Gardens

In November, 1934 the Borough Council acquired no.5 Hill Street for its new offices. The grounds attached to the offices were dedicated as a rest garden for the use of the public in March, 1935 to commemorate the Silver Jubilee of King George V and Queen Mary. A new entrance was made into Hill Street, and they were named Jubilee Gardens.

-   *Malcolm White*

Stuffed Baby Marrows with Saffron

Serves 10 – 12

This flavourful recipe is from Valencia, a port on the Spanish coast. Serve with gazpacho.

- 6 threads saffron
- 150ml boiling water
- 6-8 baby marrow or courgettes, hollowed out to thickness of your little finger. Reserve the flesh and dice.
- 4 tablespoons olive oil
- 50g chopped bacon or Serrano ham
- 100g peas
- 1 small onion, finely chopped
- 1 teaspoon dried thyme
- 1 tablespoon marjoram, chopped
- 7 tablespoons leftover rice/paella
- 1 egg, lightly beaten
- 1 lemon, finely grated zest and juice
- Salt and freshly ground pepper

Soak saffron threads for 20 minutes in boiling water. Arrange hollowed out marrows in a roasting dish, neatly without gaps.

Heat 2 tablespoons of oil in a small frying pan.

Add chopped onion, fry gently till soft and golden.

Add reserved chopped marrow, stir until soft.

Stir in ham, peas and herbs.

Season, remove from heat, leave to cool.

Mix thoroughly with rice, egg, lemon zest.

Add lemon juice to saffron water.

Preheat oven to 180°C.

Fill the marrow shells with the rice mixture.

Drizzle with oil and pour saffron water into the gaps.

Cover with foil, shiny side down.

Bake for 30-40 minutes until marrows are tender.

Remove foil, baste with saffron scented juices.

Cook for another 10 minutes until rice is crisp and golden.

Library

The Corn Exchange, a building essential for a market town serving a large rural area, was built on the site of the former Woolstaplers Hall, in 1847. It continued as the successful centre of the arable trade for over a hundred years, but with the advent of different trading methods gradually became obsolete. In 1974, the building was sold to Essex County Council who converted it into a library incorporating both the County Library and the library of the Town's Literary and Scientific Society.

- *Malcolm White*

Vegetable Paella (Vegan)

This vegetable paella is light yet filling and can be enjoyed alone or with meat, fish or chicken.

- 1 cup Arborio (risotto) rice
- ½ onion chopped
- 2 tablespoons olive oil
- 2 carrots, chopped
- ½ cup corn
- 1 cup peas
- ½ cup red pepper chopped
- ½ cup green pepper chopped
- 2 cups vegetable broth
- 1 clove garlic
- 6 threads saffron, crushed
- 1 bay leaf
- Thyme freshly ground
- black pepper and salt as needed
- 2 tablespoons chopped parsley

Heat olive oil in large frying pan on medium heat.
Cook for a few minutes.
Add carrots, corn, peas, tomatoes, peppers and garlic.
Turn down heat, cook for 7 minutes.
Add vegetable broth, bring to boil.
Add bay leaf and crushed saffron.
Combine with the cooked vegetables.
Turn heat to very low, seal the pot with foil.
Cook for 20 minutes. Season.
If rice is still moist, continue to cook uncovered
for a few minutes

The Common

The Common has existed as an open space since time immemorial. It was probably used for a tournament recorded in 1252 when two knights, Roger de Leeburn and Ernauld de Mounteney fought each other with lances, the unfortunate de Mounteney being killed. In 1972 the Common, previously almost certainly manorial waste, came into the ownership of the Borough Council. Today the Common is an essential part of the town's social life.

- *Malcolm White*

Persian Ice Cream with Saffron and Rose Water

This is a wonderfully refreshing dessert on a hot summer's day filled with the mystique of the Orient.

- 1 litre tub of vanilla ice cream
- 4 threads saffron, crushed
- 2 tablespoons boiling water
- 1 tablespoon rose water
- ½ cup shelled pistachios, coarsely chopped

Soak saffron threads for 20 minutes in boiling water.
Soften the tub of ice cream at room temperature for 20 minutes.
Place softened ice cream in a large bowl.
Add saffron, rose water and pistachios.
Mix well, till thoroughly combined.
Scrape ice cream back into the tub.
Freeze until hardened (6 hours).

Drinking Fountain

The fountain in the Market Square had originally been on show at the 1862 Exhibition in London. It was purchased by George Stacey Gibson who had it erected in the Market Square in 1863 to commemorate the marriage of the Prince of Wales (later Edward VII) and Princess Alexandra.

- *Malcolm White*

Saffron Kheer

A twist on rice pudding with nuts, cardamom and saffron. You can also use almond, soy or rice milk for this dish.

- 80g blanched almonds
- 30g rice grains
- 1.25 litres milk (5 cups)
- 6 threads saffron
- 80g caster sugar
- ½ teaspoon cardamom powder

Soak rice grains for 30 minutes until smooth.
Blend almonds, rice and 250ml milk.
Boil remaining 200ml milk and saffron.
Reduce heat, simmer for 15 minutes.
Pour in blended ingredients, stir until mixture thickens.
Stir in sugar and cardamom and simmer until sugar dissolves.
Serve warm or cold.

Market Square

Saffron Walden first acquired its market in 1141. Originally the market was held in what are now the museum grounds. But over the years as the town developed, the Market Square became the home of the twice weekly market. It is held every Tuesday and Saturday.

-   *Malcolm White*

Saffron Panna Cotta (Custard)

This Italian recipe offers a twist on custard, lightly spiced with saffron. Garnish with nuts or edible petals... a sprinkling of nutmeg or cinnamon...

- ¼ cup cold water
- 1 sheet gelatine
- ½ cup sugar
- 3 threads saffron
- ¼ teaspoon almond extract
- 1 ½ cups heavy cream
- 1 cup milk

Soak saffron threads for 20 minutes in hot milk.
Put water in a small bowl, place gelatine on top, let it stand for 5minutes or until soft.
Add cream, saffron, milk and sugar to a saucepan.
Bring just to boil on medium heat, while stirring constantly.
Remove from heat.
Add soft gelatine, stir until completely dissolved.
Stir in almond extract.
Pour mixture into a medium bowl.
Place in a larger bowl of ice water.
Stir often with a rubber spatula until the mixture cools (about 20 minutes).
Pour into 6 dessert dishes.
Cover with cling film.
Refrigerate for 4 hours.

Uttlesford District Council Offices- Old Saffron Walden Hospital, London Road

Originally designed as a hospital by the Quaker architect William Beck, this beautiful High Victorian Gothic style building was opened in 1865. Its red and white brickwork features stone dressings and gothic windows, an open stone porch and the steeply pitched roof covered in fish scale bands and cresting. Granite piers support the structure. A stone fleur-de-lis tops all the gables. The stone plaque beneath the eaves is inscribed "S WALDEN G HOSPITAL". The hospital was funded with a sum of money bequeathed by the Quaker, Wyatt George Gibson, who died in 1862.

Saffron Pineapple Halwa

A fruity, nutty dessert full of colour and flavour.

- 100ml melted ghee (clarified butter)
- 220g semolina
- 300g canned pineapple
- 10 threads saffron
- 650ml water
- Syrup from pineapple
- ¼ teaspoon salt
- 200g caster sugar
- 12 cardamom pods, pounded
- 80g cashew nuts chopped and roasted
- 80g raisins fried in ghee
- 300g canned pineapple, coarsely chopped

Heat ghee and lightly fry semolina until fragrant.
Bring water, pineapple syrup, saffron salt to the boil.
Pour syrup mixture with semolina into a non-stick pan, stirring constantly over low heat until mixture thickens to form a paste.
Stir in nuts, raisins and pineapple
Spoon halwa into a greased tray, spread evenly.
Allow to cool.
Scoop into small plates as dessert.

Town Hall

Originally built in 1761 on the site of The Dolphin, a public house and some small tenements, the Town Hall was extended, and a new Court Room added, in 1879. The Town Hall has been largely used as a social centre, with the Magistrates Court moving out in 1979. It also houses the Tourist Information Centre. The roof and the structure has been painstakingly and sensitively restored in 2016.

- *Malcolm White*

Carrot and Saffron Cake

Serves 12

This carrot cake recipe is actually my daughter, Katie's. It is quick and easy to make and is always a hit. It is my favourite cake. Slather the icing on thickly, then decorate with nuts.

- 6 threads saffron
- 2 tablespoons of boiling water
- 625g cake flour
- 10ml baking powder
- 7.5ml bicarbonate of soda
- Pinch of salt
- 5ml cinnamon
- 4 eggs, beaten
- 375g sugar
- 310ml oil
- 750g grated carrots

Soak saffron threads for 20 minutes in boiling water.
Sift dry ingredients twice.
Cream eggs and sugar.
Add oil, saffron and mix.
Fold egg mixture, then carrots into dry ingredients.
Place mixture in a greased cake tin.
Bake at 180°C for 45 minutes.

Icing

Beat together 60g butter, 800g icing sugar, 150g smooth cottage cheese, 2.5ml vanilla essence and 2.5ml lemon juice.

Pig Market

The Pig Market (or more originally the Borough Market) was created in 1831, on the site of the former Eight Bells pub. Originally intended for the sale of horses and cattle, until then sold in the Market Square, it later sold mainly small animals and poultry with larger animals being sold in the new cattle market. Its use as a market declined rapidly in the 1970s and it was redeveloped in the early 1980's.

- *Malcolm White*

Christmas Fruit Cake with Saffron

Serves 12

This recipe is my signature Christmas cake dating back to when I first got married in Johannesburg and attended a cooking course which included this recipe. It changes depending on the nuts I have at hand and how liberally I add the spices. It has been baked as wedding cakes for family and friends and shipped across the seas at Christmas time.

- 30g glazed cherries, sliced
- 60g dates sliced
- 500g mixed dried fruit
- 250g butter
- 1 tin sweetened condensed milk
- 250ml water
- 5ml bicarbonate of soda
- 1 egg
- 300g flour
- A pinch of salt
- 2ml nutmeg
- 2ml mixed spice
- 6 threads saffron
- 10ml boiling water
- 200g almonds, chopped
- 200g hazelnuts, chopped
- 200g walnuts, chopped

Soak saffron threads for 20 minutes in boiling water.
Boil the first 6 ingredients together for 3 minutes.
Allow to cool.
Add bicarbonate of soda and mix well.
Beat egg add to mixture and mix well.
Add sifted dry ingredients, nuts and saffron mixture.
Mix well and place mixture in a greased lined baking tin.
Bake for 2 and1/2 hours at 150°C.

Saffron Hall

Saffron Hall is a world-class concert hall with world-class acoustics. It sits at the heart of the excellent Saffron Walden County High School and is well loved and appreciated by both the pupils of the school and the local community. Every week students, their families, local residents and people throughout the region can engage with some of the world's finest musicians and artists by attending an event, performing at the hall with local groups or participating in one of the many projects available. Saffron Walden has always been a hub of cultural activity. The strong community is fuelled by the love of making music, drama and art together and that in turn strengthens the great bond the residents enjoy amongst themselves.

-   Angela Dickson

Mince Pies (Christmas)

The soft, buttery texture of these mince pies will melt in your mouth. I am told that these are the best mince pies (particularly by people not fond of them). Here saffron is used in the glaze to give the pies a golden and festive glaze.

- 250g butter
- 250g flour
- 1 tablespoon caster sugar
- 1 egg separated
- 1 tablespoon vinegar
- 3 tablespoon iced water
- 1 glass minced fruit mix
- 3 threads saffron
- 50ml hot milk

Soak saffron threads in hot milk for 20 minutes.
Mix butter into flour.
Add sugar.
Mix beaten egg yolk, vinegar and water.
In a separate cup, add saffron to milk.
Mix egg mixture into flour mixture
Place pastry in fridge for 2 hours.
Roll out pastry (3mm thick), cut into circles with cookie cutters.
Line the bottom of each mould in the muffin tin with a circle.
Place 1 tablespoon of minced fruit on each base.
Close with a pastry circle lid.
Press down the sides with a fork to seal.
Prick each lid twice with a fork.
Baste each mince pie with saffron milk mixture.
Bake at 200°C for 20 minutes.

Church Street

Church Street was laid out with Castle Street and the Castle in the 1140s, and joins up the Castle, Church and High Street. The street is dominated by the series of three buildings, collectively known as the Sun Inn. Two are hall houses, of about 1340, and all are decorated, to varying degrees, with pargetting. Some of the pargetting is quite simple, but the most elaborate, possibly dating back to 1676 (one of four dates on the buildings), show fruit and animals. On the main feature, there are two figures in 17th century costume thought to be either Gog and Magog, or Tom Hickerthrift and the Wisbeach Giant. The debate continues...

- *Sarah Kirkpatrick*

Saffron Honey Syrup Cakes

These honey syrup cakes have a transformative quality, eliciting a joyous reaction from the recipient every time. This has been the most surprisingly delicious saffron recipe I have found to date. Try it and see...

- 4 threads saffron
- 2 teaspoons lemon rind, finely grated
- 2 teaspoons lemon juice
- Seeds from 1 vanilla pod
- 150g caster sugar
- 150g butter, softened
- 250g flour
- 2 teaspoons baking powder
- 250g Greek yoghurt
- Whipped Greek yoghurt
- 55g pistachios coarsely chopped

For the syrup

- Vanilla bean reserved from cakes
- 90g honey
- 180ml water
- 2 strips lemon rind
- 6 cloves
- 2 cinnamon sticks

Mix saffron and lemon juice, for 20 minutes.
Preheat oven to 180°C. Grease a muffin tray.
Beat butter, sugar, vanilla seeds and lemon rind in a small bowl until pale and fluffy - 3 minutes.
Beat in yolks, one at a time until smooth.
Transfer to a large bowl. Sift flour and baking powder in another bowl.
Stir the flour and yoghurt in 2 batches then stir in saffron mixture.
Beat egg whites in a small bowl to stiff peaks.
Stir beaten egg whites into cake mixture in two batches.
Spoon mixture into each pan hole.
Bake for 25 minutes, until skewer comes out cleanly.

Honey saffron syrup

Add all syrup ingredients to a small saucepan.
Stir over medium heat until sugar dissolves.
Bring to boil. Remove from heat, stand for 5 minutes.
Discard whole spices.
Turn hot cakes onto a wire rack over an oven tray.
Drizzle hot syrup over hot cakes; allow syrup to soak into cakes.
Serve with whipped yoghurt and nuts.

Friends Meeting House

This House is a large red building in High Street that does not have a house number. It is where Quakers in Saffron Walden meet - Quakers are also known as Friends. The building is simple and comfortable, has several rooms with a disabled access. It has a garden that is usually open to the public. It is a peaceful place to be. The Meeting House is used by local groups for a variety of activities that range from art to yoga.

Saffron Eggless Biscuits Laced with Pistachios

Serves 6 – 12

These biscuits are really tasty and can be prepared in 10 minutes, a nice change from choc chip.

- 4 threads saffron, crushed to a paste
- 1 tablespoon hot milk (to infuse saffron)
- 6 cardamom pods, ground
- ¼ teaspoon nutmeg, ground
- 20 crushed/chopped pistachios
- 200g flour
- 100g butter
- 115g caster sugar

Infuse saffron in hot milk for 20 minutes.
Mix sugar and butter together well (use blender).
Add saffron, nutmeg and cardamom, blend.
Add flour, mix well to form dough.
(You may need to add a few more drops of milk).
Roll half the dough into a 6" circle.
Sprinkle half the pistachios over it and lightly embed the pistachios by rolling over the dough again.
Repeat using all the dough.
Cut out biscuits with a cookie cutter.
Place on baking paper on a baking tray.
Bake at 175°C for 10-15 minutes.

The Rows

This corner site dating from the late 15th century has a jetty (the upper floor overhang on a timber- framed building) that provides visual impact and protects goods and shoppers from the rain. Three clear sections can be seen: large Tudor windows for displaying goods and providing light for the craftsman's workshop, the open hall in the middle and the roof that was raised in the 18th century. The Rows included 33 of the 46 medieval shops of the town's shopping centre sited there in 1630.

Saffron Oaties

These golden oaties are perfect for unexpected guests, lunch boxes, picnics and road trips. They can also be baked in muffin tins.

- 4 threads saffron
- 2 tablespoons boiling water
- 250g butter
- 2 tablespoons Golden Syrup
- 2 tablespoons bicarbonate of soda
- 1 cup flour
- 2 cups coconut
- 2 cups oats
- 1 cup sugar

Soak saffron threads for 20 minutes in boiling water.
Mix and heat butter, syrup bicarbonate and saffron in a saucepan/ microwave.
Mix dry ingredients together.
Make a well in the dry ingredients.
Add liquid and mix well.
Press and smooth mixture into a greased baking tray.
Bake at 170°C for 15 - 20 minutes until golden brown.

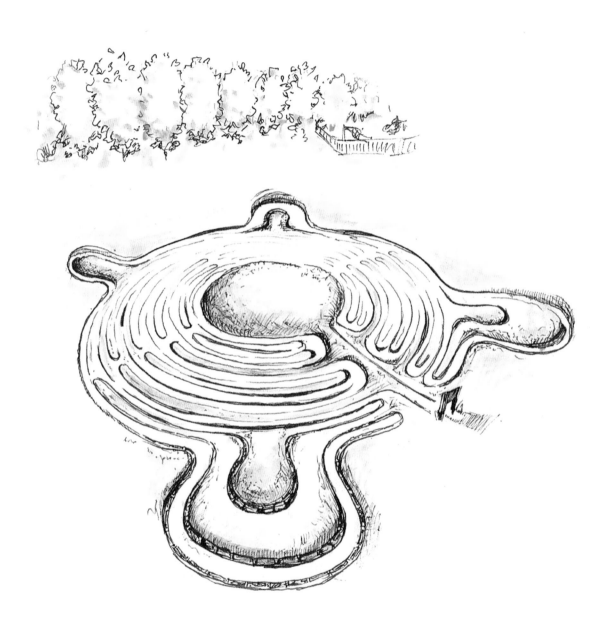

Turf Maze

The origins or aims of the turf maze on the eastern end of the Common are unknown. The earliest record relating to the maze details its cutting in 1699. The maze, the largest publicly owned maze in the country, was recut in 1911, and the bricks marking the path were dug up and relaid in 1978.

- *Malcolm White*

Saffron Polenta and Orange Cake

Serves 12

This Italian cake can be served with ice cream or a compote of winter fruits spiced with cinnamon or pears in wine.

- 175g flour
- 1 teaspoon baking powder
- 50g polenta
- 6 threads saffron
- 3 tablespoons boiling water
- 225ml walnut/mild olive oil
- 4 medium eggs
- 2 Seville oranges or 1 orange and zest and juice of 1 lemon

Soak saffron threads for 20 mintes in boiling water.
Sift flour and baking powder.
Add polenta and sugar, toss lightly to mix.
Make a well in the middle, add oil and eggs.
Add saffron mixture.
Mix with a wooden spoon till smooth.
Add orange/lemon zest and juice; mixture should drop from spoon, add a little water if the mixture is too stiff.
Drop mixture into a greased 18cm square tin.
Line base with baking paper brushed with orange juice. Smooth into corners, flatten the top.
Bake at 170°C for 1 ¼ hours (check after an hour, sides should have shrunk.
Let it rest for 10 minutes.
Transfer to wire tray to cool.
Peel off paper.

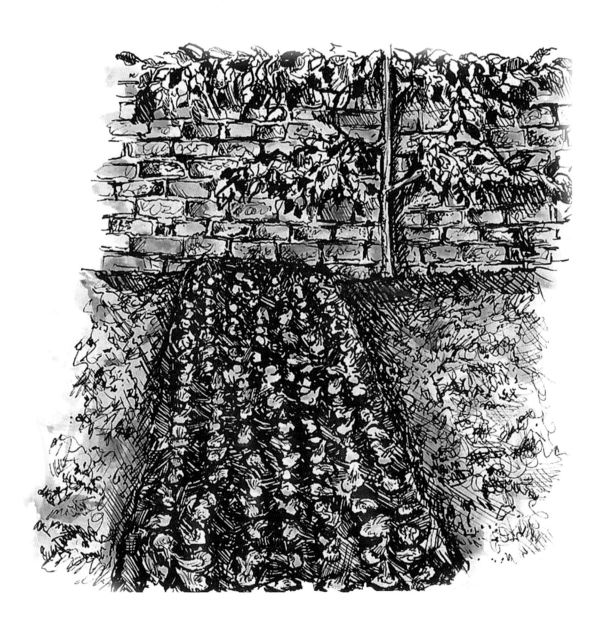

Crocus Beds in Bridge End Gardens

Six hundred corms (bulbs) of the crocus species Crocus Sativus were planted in Bridge End Gardens Walled Garden in October 2016 to remind us of the crop that played such an interesting role as a dye, a foodstuff, a medicine and a cosmetic in the Town's history. Cultivation of the saffron crocus was concentrated around Walden for 200 years from the 15th Century to later in the 17th century. After flowering in the autumn, the threads were removed, dried in kilns and pressed into 'cake' for sale as a dye or medicine. A fair used to be held in Saffron Walden on October 31st and in Newport on November 17th.

Saffron Shortbread

This simple recipe works for me every time and is a firm favourite of my sisters. The texture is light and crumbly and the added saffron gives it an interesting nuance.

- 4 threads saffron
- 2 tablespoons boiling water
- 225g cornflour
- 225g flour
- 250g soft butter
- 110g caster sugar
- 150g currants

Soak saffron threads for 20 minutes in boiling water.
Sift cornflour and flour.
Rub butter into dry ingredients.
Add saffron, caster sugar and currants.
Knead until soft dough is formed.
Press dough into 20cm x 29cm baking tray.
Mark the slices lightly and prick with a fork.
Bake at 160°C for 1 hour.
Allow the shortbread to cool before turning out.
Dredge with additional caster sugar.

Bibliography

1. Everett, M & Stewart, D: The Buildings of Saffron Walden
2. Francis, S Dr: Saffron 2011
3. Luard, E: Saffron and Sunshine 2000
4. Singh DJ: the Magic of Saffron 2015
5. White, M: Saffron Walden's History: A Chronological Compilation 1991 (Pages47-49)